Homemade Niche Products

Recipes

Niche Categories

- Automobile
- Perfumes
- Pet Care
- Cleaning
- Home Repair

Shahaan Merchant

HOMEMADE NICHE PRODUCTS RECIPES

Automobile Care, Pet Care, Home Repair, Perfumes & Fragrance, Washing & Cleaning

Author
Shahaan Merchant

Copyright

All rights reserved. No part of this publication may be reproduced, distributed, or transmitted in any form or by any means, including photocopying, recording, or other electronic or mechanical methods, without the prior written permission of the publisher, except in the case of brief quotations embodied in critical reviews and certain other noncommercial uses permitted by copyright law.

This book is intended for personal use and informational purposes only. The recipes, formulations, methods, and instructions provided herein are the intellectual property of the authors and are protected under copyright law. Any unauthorized reproduction, distribution, or adaptation of the content, in whole or in part, is strictly prohibited and may result in legal action.

Disclaimer

The information provided in this book is for educational and informational purposes only. The recipes, instructions, and formulations shared are based on research and experience but are not guaranteed to be error-free, accurate, or suitable for all individuals or circumstances.While every effort has been made to ensure accuracy, the authors and publishers cannot be held responsible for any adverse reactions, accidents, or damages that may arise from the use, misuse, or application of the information contained herein.

Readers understand and acknowledge that the creation, application, or use of homemade products described in this book carries inherent risks. The authors, publishers, and affiliated parties do not assume any responsibility or liability for the accuracy, completeness, suitability, or outcomes resulting from the utilization of the information presented herein.

Furthermore, the authors and publishers disclaim any responsibility for:

Allergic reactions, skin irritations, or adverse health effects resulting from the use of homemade products, as individual sensitivities vary.

Accidents, damages, or injuries incurred during the production, application, or storage of homemade products.

Any inaccuracies, omissions, or errors in the recipes, formulations, or instructions provided.

Readers are strongly advised to:

Conduct patch tests and seek professional advice before using any homemade products, especially if they have known allergies, sensitivities, or health conditions.

Perform thorough research, including cross-referencing multiple sources, to ensure the safety, suitability, and legality of ingredients and methods used.

Adhere to safety guidelines, including proper storage, handling of ingredients, and compliance with local regulations and laws concerning product manufacturing and distribution.

By using the information in this book, readers agree to hold harmless the authors, publishers, and affiliates from any liability, claims, damages, or expenses that may arise directly or indirectly from the use or misuse of the provided information.

Table of Contents

Beeswax Candles
Furniture Polish
Wood Polish
Wood Stain
Wood Preservative
Tile and Grout cleaner

Perfumes & Fragrance

SIMPLE ALCOHOL-BASED Perfume
Room Spray
Air Freshener
Essential Oil Blend
Incense Sticks
Reed Diffusers
Deodorant
Solid Perfume

Washing & Cleaning

DISHWASHING LIQUID
Laundry Detergent
Fabric Softener
All Purpose Cleaner
Glass Cleaner
Toilet Bowl Cleaner
Carpet Cleaner
Leather Cleaner and Conditioner
Metal Polish
Rust Remover
Beeswax Wraps

Understanding the nature and properties of ingredients before diving into making products from these recipes is crucial for several reasons:

Safety and Effectiveness

UNDERSTANDING HOW EACH ingredient acts and interacts with others means your homemade products will be safe and effective. Knowing their characteristics prevents dangerous blends or reactions which could make the product worthless or worse, unsafe.

Allergies and Sensitivities

SOME PEOPLE MAY BE allergic or sensitive to particular ingredients. Knowing these things will help you decide what else to use, or do patch tests first to make sure your products are safe for anybody who might use them.

Product Performance

DIFFERENT INGREDIENTS have different effects and roles in a formula. Knowing these properties is important in designing formulations to get what's wanted. For example, learning which oils provide moisture, which act as preservatives, and which give a scent can help you create products that work well.

Sustainability and Eco-friendliness

KNOWING ABOUT INGREDIENTS makes it possible to choose environmentally friendly options. Some could be more sustainable or have a smaller ecological footprint, making them more in line with your ideals and supporting a more eco friendly lifestyle.

Cost-effectiveness

KNOWING THE PROPERTIES of ingredients makes it easier to choose wisely and make sound investments, that is to invest in ingredients which can be used in a variety of dishes. This can save money in the long run by cutting down on waste and raising utility levels.

Customization and Innovation

ONCE YOU KNOW ABOUT properties, you can experiment and come up with your own formulas. Understanding the behavior of each ingredient allows for creative adjustments and substitutions, resulting in unique and personal products.

Legal and Regulatory Compliance

IN SOME AREAS THERE may be ingredient restrictions or regulations which you must be aware of. Some ingredients may be subject to legal restrictions, or require special handling, and being aware of these ahead of time avoids complications.

In essence, understanding the type and properties of ingredients is essential to making safe, effective and individualized products. It allows you to make enlightened choices, formulations that are perfect for your needs, and you can have extra peace of mind because the products you produce aren't just practical-they're also safe for you and those around you.

Liquid Castile Soap

This soft soap, made from vegetable oils, is a seasoning in many cleaning formulations. Because it is a natural, biodegradable material, this makes it an excellent fit for car shampoos, pet shampoos, dishwashing liquid and even all-purpose cleaners. Soft and mild, it cleans without harsh chemicals.

White Vinegar

BECAUSE OF ITS ACIDIC nature, this kitchen staple also serves as a strong cleaning agent. Due to its disinfectant and degreasing properties, it's extremely common in glass cleaners, all-purpose cleaners, and even some pet care products.

Essential Oils

THESE HIGHLY CONCENTRATED oils are extracted from plants, not only give off wonderful aromas but also possess natural antibacterial, antifungal and aromatic properties. They make a completely natural addition to homemade perfumes, room sprays, cleaners and pet care products, with pleasant but sometimes therapeutic scents.

Beeswax

BEESWAX, WHICH IS WELL known for its protective properties, works as a natural emulsifier and thickener. It is commonly found in furniture polishes, wood preservatives, and balms, providing a protective coating along with a glossy sheen.

Soy Wax Flakes

MADE FROM SOYBEANS, this environmentally friendly substitute for paraffin wax is frequently found in candles. It burns cleaner and longer, scenes well, so it is a popular choice for homemade candle recipes.

Carnauba Wax

CARNAUBA WAX IS SOURCED from palm leaves. It is one of the hardest waxy materials, and gives an excellent high-gloss finish. A common additive to car waxes and polishes, it provides durable protection and shine to automotive surfaces.

Jojoba Oil

BECAUSE IT IS LIKE human sebum, jojoba oil is an excellent moisturizer. Its nourishing and conditioning capabilities are found in pet care products, cosmetics, and sometimes even car care solutions.

Coconut Oil

IT HAS CLEANSING PROPERTIES by nature and is used in a lot of cleaning solutions because it easily cuts through grease and grime. Besides, its pleasant fragrance makes it a common ingredient in handmade soaps and pet products.

Vegetable Glycerin

VEGETABLE GLYCERIN is a humectant, retaining moisture in products. This common ingredient in soaps, shampoos and pet care products keeps skin and fur moist.

Liquid Dish Soap

ESPECIALLY EFFECTIVE at cutting greases, liquid dish soap is an important component of dishwashing liquids, all-purpose cleaners, and even some pet shampoos.

Isopropyl Alcohol (Rubbing Alcohol)

THIS IS A STRONG ANTISEPTIC and evaporates rapidly. Its original form was much used in room sprays, perfumes, and some cleaning solutions.

Baking Soda

VERSATILE IN CLEANING solutions, baking soda is mildly abrasive and deodorizing. It cleans and deodorizes surfaces very effectively without scratching.

Citrus Essential Oil

THIS OIL IS DERIVED from citrus fruits and it has a fresh, clean scent. It also has natural cleansing properties. It's a common ingredient in many cleaning fluids, air fresheners and perfumes.

Coffee Grounds

COFFEE GROUNDS ARE well known for their abrasive texture, which makes them great for scrubbing and deodorizing. Sometimes they are used in cleaning products to fight the most difficult stains.

Hydrogen Peroxide

HYDROGEN PEROXIDE IS an excellent disinfectant and bleaching agent, able to remove stains and is often found in homemade cleaners and stain removers.

Witch Hazel

SUCH A NATURAL ASTRINGENT is used in pet care products and perfumes because it has a calming and cleansing effect, especially on the skin.

Peppermint Essential Oil

WITH ITS FRESH SCENT and antimicrobial properties, peppermint oil is added to cleaning agents and personal care products for its clean scent and perhaps germ-fighting abilities.

Tea Tree Essential Oil

TEA TREE OIL IS AN active antibacterial and antifungal product. It is frequently the basis of many cleaning products, as well as pet care items, and even skincare formulations.

Eucalyptus Essential Oil

BECAUSE OF ITS CLEAN and crisp scent, along with its antibacterial properties, eucalyptus oil is often added to cleaning solutions, room sprays, and even sometimes in home-made insect repellents.

Wood Powder or Sawdust

WOOD POWDER OR SAWDUST When added to wood polishes or fillers, they absorb oils and create smooth finishes, especially when combined with other ingredients.

Makko Powder or Gum Arabic

MAKKO POWDER, ALSO known as gum arabic, is used as a binding agent in incense sticks and air fresheners. It holds fragrances in place and shapes the product.

Super Washing Soda

SUPER WASHING SODA Super washing soda is a booster in laundry and general cleaners. It softens water, removes stains, and cleans even the most difficult surfaces.

Borax

IN MANY CLEANING PRODUCTS, borax serves as a cleaning agent, a stain remover and a deodorizer. It breaks down dirt and neutralizes odors.

Bay Leaves

BAY LEAVES ARE KNOWN for their fragrance and are also sometimes used in cleaning agents to give them a pleasing fragrance.

Cornstarch or Arrowroot Powder

THICKENERS FOUND IN many recipes that give body and texture to products such as deodorants and powders.

Toothpaste

TOOTHPASTE IS SOMETIMES used in cleaning solutions as a mildly abrasive scrubbing agent.

Car Wax

MADE JUST FOR AUTOMOBILES, car wax protects and shines up the exteriors of cars.

Polishing Compound

THESE ABRASIVE PASTES or liquids help polishing tools smooth and shine surfaces.

Mineral Spirits or Naphtha

OILS, WAXES AND GREASES are dissolved by these solvents, and are often found in cleaning products and polishes.

Aloe Vera Gel

ALOE VERA GEL IS COMMONLY used in skincare and pet care for its calming and emollient qualities. It heals wounds and relieves skin irritations.

Apple Cider Vinegar

BECAUSE OF ITS ACETIC acid, apple cider vinegar is used in cleaning solutions and in caring for pets because of its antibacterial properties.

Lavender Essential Oil

WITH ITS CALMING SCENT and possible antibacterial properties, this oil is commonly included in cleaning and personal care products.

Shea Butter, Sweet Almond Oil, Olive Oil, Vitamin E Oil

FOR THESE NATURAL OILS and butters, their moisturizing and conditioning effects on skin and fur find application in many skincare and pet care products.

Oat Flour or Ground Oats

OAT FLOUR, USED IN skincare products to exfoliate gently and soothe the skin, is quite calming to irritated skin.

Ingredients:

- Liquid Castile Soap - 1/4 cup

- White Vinegar - 1/4 cup

- Warm Water - 1 gallon

- Essential Oils - 10-15 drops (optional, for fragrance and added cleaning properties)

Equipment/Tools:

- Bucket or container for mixing
- Soft sponge or microfiber wash mitt
- Hose or bucket of clean water for rinsing
- Towels for drying

Method:

Prepare Your Workspace:

The work environment should be clean and dry. Collect all the ingredients and tools required.

Mix the Ingredients:

IN A BUCKET OR CONTAINER, mix liquid castile soap, white vinegar, and warm water. Mix thoroughly, to make sure the ingredients are combined.

Optional: Add Essential Oils:

IF DESIRED, YOU MAY add 10 or 15 drops of fragrance-creating essential oils to the mixture for further cleaning power. Some essential oils, such as lemon or tea tree, may also be effective for their cleansing properties.

Wash the Car:

CLEAN THE CAR WITH clean water, which will wash away loose segments of dirt and debris.

Wipe the surface of your car down with homemade car shampoo using a soft sponge or microfiber wash mitt. Break it up into sections, for example, from top to bottom.

Rinse Thoroughly:

AFTER WASHING EACH section thoroughly with clean water, wash again to remove shampoo residue.

Dry the Car:

BE SURE TO USE CLEAN towels to dry the surface of the car to avoid leaving water spots.

Additional Tips:

- Usage: This homemade car shampoo can be used to wash your vehicle. Yet it is gentle enough so it can be used repeatedly without damaging the paint.

- Adjustments: The amount of essential oils can be changed to suit your taste or left out entirely.

THE RESULTING CAR SHAMPOO is a simple concoction that offers a naturally effective method of cleaning your car. Do a patch test on a small area to determine suitability. Tailor the ingredients to your own taste and the requirements of your vehicle.

Ingredients:

- Beeswax - 1 cup (grated or chopped finely)

- Carnauba Wax - 1/2 cup (grated or chopped finely)

- Jojoba Oil - 1/4 cup

- Coconut Oil - 1/4 cup

- Essential Oils - 10-15 drops (optional, for fragrance and added protection)

Equipment/Tools:

- Double boiler or makeshift one (a pot and heat-resistant container)
- Stirring utensil (metal spoon or wooden stick)
- Airtight container for storage

Method:

Prepare Your Workspace:
Keep your work area clean and dry. Collect all the necessary ingredients and utensils.

Melt the Waxes and Oils:

Heat over low to medium heat, combining the beeswax, carnauba wax, jojoba oil and coconut oil in a double boiler (or a pot with a heat-resistant container inside). Continue stirring occasionally until the mixture is completely melted and combined.

Optional: Add Essential Oils:

If desired, add 10-15 drops of essential oils for fragrance and added protection. Some essential oils such as lemon or lavender can be helpful and have added preserved properties.

Transfer to Storage Container:

Let the pour the wax mixture into an airtight storage container. Then let it cool to a solid.

How to Use:

USE THE INCLUDED SOFT cloth or applicator pad to apply the car wax to your vehicle's exterior.

We then work in small sections, using circular motions to apply the wax.

Let the wax dry to a haze (according to the drying time indicated on the wax).

Then use a clean, dry cloth to buff off the haze to achieve a brilliant effect.

Additional Tips:

- Usage: This do-it-your-self car wax will keep your vehicle's paint bright and shiny.

- Storage: The car wax should be kept in a cool, dry place, which will preserve the consistency.

THIS DO-IT-YOURSELF car wax provides a natural protective layer for your automobile. Never forget to first try in a small area to make sure they are compatible with your vehicle's paint. Tweak the ingredients to suit your taste and the condition of your car's paint.

Ingredients:

- Jojoba Oil - 1/2 cup
- Vegetable Glycerin - 1/4 cup
- White Vinegar - 1/4 cup
- Liquid Dish Soap - 2 tablespoons
- Water - 2 cups
- Essential Oils - 10-15 drops (optional, for fragrance)

Equipment/Tools:

- Mixing bowl or container
- Spray bottle or applicator pad

Method:

Prepare Your Workspace:

Keep your work area neat and dry. Collect all the necessary ingredients and tools.

Mix the Ingredients:

Pour the jojoba oil, vegetable glycerin, white vinegar, liquid dish soap, water, and essential oils into a mixing bowl or container. Mix the ingredients thoroughly, stirring or shaking as needed.

Transfer to a Spray Bottle or Applicator:

Mix the homemade tire shine and pour into a spray bottle. Or you can apply it with an applicator pad or sponge.

How to Use:

GIVE THE SPRAY BOTTLE a good shake first.

Spray homemade tires shine onto a clean tire surface, or use an applicator pad.

Rub it evenly over the tire by spreading it out.

Let it completely dry before driving the vehicle.

Additional Tips:

● Usage: This homemade tire shine serves as a quick fix to make your vehicle's tires look good and shiny.

● Adjustments: The only difference is, you can change the amounts of the essential oils for the ideal aroma, or omit them entirely.

IT'S A DO-IT-YOURSELF tire shine that uses a natural product to beautify your car's tires. Test a small area at all times for compatibility. Adjust the ingredients accordingly to suit both your tastes and the requirements of your tires.

Ingredients:

- Distilled Water - 1 gallon

- Isopropyl Alcohol (Rubbing Alcohol) - 1 quart

- Liquid Dish Soap - 1 tablespoon

- Optional: Vinegar - 1/2 cup (for added cleaning power, especially for removing bugs and grime)

Equipment/Tools:

- Large container or jug for mixing
- Funnel for pouring into washer fluid reservoir

Method:

Prepare Your Workspace:
Keep your work area clean and dry. Collect all the necessary ingredients and equipment.

Mix the Ingredients:

Pour the distilled water and isopropyl alcohol into a large container or jug. Mix thoroughly by stirring or shaking.

Add Dish Soap and Optional Vinegar:

Then add the liquid dish soap and softly mix it in.

Vinegar is also added for an extra cleansing ability. Mix thoroughly.

Transfer to Washer Fluid Reservoir:

Pour the homemade windshield washer fluid into the vehicle's washer fluid tank with a funnel.

How to Use:

YOU WOULD USE IT JUST as you do any commercial windshield washer fluid with your vehicle's windshield wipers and washer system.

Additional Tips:

- Usage: When driving, spray this homemade windshield washer fluid on your vehicle's windshield in order to clean off dirt, grime, and bugs.

- Adjustments: You can change the proportions to be a little less or a little more for this, but you shouldn't increase the alcohol concentration too much. Otherwise, it will be harmful to some finishes or paints.

THIS DO-IT-YOURSELF windshield washer fluid becomes a cheap and practical substitute. You should always refer to your car's owner's manual to see whether or not it can be used, though in general they should be compatible with the windshield washer system. Vehicle changes, adjust ingredients to suit.

Ingredients:

- Baking Soda - 1 cup

- Liquid Dish Soap - 1/4 cup

- White Vinegar - 1/4 cup

- Water - 1 gallon

- Optional: Citrus Essential Oil - 10-15 drops (for added degreasing power and fragrance)

Equipment/Tools:

- Large container or bucket for mixing
- Spray bottle or pump sprayer
- Protective gloves and eyewear (optional but recommended)

Method:

Prepare Your Workspace:
Ventilate your work area, and be sure to protect the paintwork of any parts of the car you don't want to get wet.

Mix the Ingredients:

Add the baking soda, liquid dish soap, white vinegar, and water to a large container or bucket. Thoroughly stir to mix thoroughly to make sure all ingredients are blended.

Optional: Add Citrus Essential Oil:

Citrus essential oil is highly degreasing and fragrant; if desired, add 10 to 15 drops to the mixture. Lemon or orange citrus oils are good options.

Transfer to a Spray Bottle or Pump Sprayer:

Then, pour the homemade engine degreaser into a spray bottle or pump sprayer so it is easy to use.

How to Use:

WAIT UNTIL THE ENGINE is cool, then spray on the degreaser.

Then liberally spray the homemade degreaser onto the engine and any grimy or greasy spots.

Allow the degreaser to soak for a few minutes to penetrate and dissolve the grease.

If areas are stubborn, use a brush or sponge to agitate.

Hose down with a hose or pressure washer and then rinse off with water. Take care not to exert excessive pressure, particularly in close proximity to sensitive parts.

Additional Tips:

- It can remove the grease and dirt that accumulates in your car's engine and its oilier areas.

- Safety Precautions: Be sure to wear protective gloves and eyewear and not to touch the degreaser with bare skin.

OUR OWN HOME-MADE ENGINE cleaner is not only good for the engine but for the environment too. Also, be certain the engine is absolutely cool before applying the degreaser and be careful about electrical components. Modify the ingredients to suit your taste and the requirements of your car.

Ingredients:

- White vinegar
- Olive oil or coconut oil
- Essential oil (optional for fragrance)

Tools:

- Mixing bowl
- Measuring cups
- Soft microfiber cloth

Method:

Prepare the Mixture: In a bowl, combine equal quantities of white vinegar and olive oil (or coconut oil). For instance, begin with 1 variety of each, 12 cups each.

Add Fragrance (Optional): You can add a few drops of your favorite essential oil if you want your polish to have a fragrance. You could use lavender or citrus oils.

Mix Thoroughly: Mix thoroughly until ingredients are well blended. The consistency should be a little thick.

Application: Polish with a soft microfiber cloth to complete the process. Dip a corner of the cloth into the mixture and rub the dashboard in circular motions.

Buffing: Then rub with a part of the cloth that hasn't been dipped in the polish to remove any excess, and buff the dashboard to a shine.

Store Remaining Mixture: Any polish leftover should be placed in an airtight container for future use.

Tips:

- Before applying it to the dashboard, test the polish on a small unnoticeable spot on the dashboard to make certain that it won't damage or stain it.

- The ingredients will separate over time, so shake or stir the mixture before using.

THERE'S NO NEED TO use harsh chemicals to polish your car's dashboard; this homemade paste will get your dashboard clean and shiny. It's inexpensive and easy to make, and it can be produced in quantities small enough to meet the needs of the individual.

Ingredients:

- 1 cup distilled water
- 1 cup white vinegar
- 2 tablespoons rubbing alcohol (optional)
- 1 tablespoon cornstarch or arrowroot powder (for added polish)
- Essential oil (optional, for fragrance)

Tools:

- Spray bottle
- Measuring cup/spoons
- Lint-free microfiber cloth

Method:

Combine the Ingredients: Combine the distilled water, white vinegar, and rubbing alcohol (if using) in a spray bottle.

Add Polishing Agent (Optional): For more polishing effect, mix in a tablespoon of cornstarch or arrowroot. This promotes a sparkling effect.

Add Fragrance (Optional): If you wish to add fragrance, add a few drops of your favorite essential oil. Citrus oils such as lemon or orange are suitable for this purpose.

Shake Well: Cover the spray bottle tightly and shake vigorously to mix well.

Application: Apply the homemade glass polish to the surface of the glass to be polished.

Wipe and Polish: Wipe the glass with a lint-free microfiber cloth, using circular motions, until dry and shining.

Buffing: To finish, polish with a clean, dry microfiber cloth for a brilliant shine.

Tips:

- To be on the safe side, first test the homemade glass polish on a corner of the glass to see whether or not it damages the latter and leaves stains.

- First shake the spray bottle to mix the ingredients thoroughly before use.

THIS DO-IT-YOURSELF glass polish is a green, economical alternative to conventional pre-made glass cleaner. Not requiring a large production plant, it is easy to make in small quantities at home, being suitable for small-scale production or even individual use.

Ingredients/Items Needed:

- Toothpaste (preferably non-gel)
- Baking soda
- Water
- Microfiber cloth
- Masking tape
- Car wax (optional)
- Polishing compound (optional)

Tools:

- Microfiber cloth
- Masking tape

Method:

Prepare the Mixture: Add a little toothpaste to a bowl with an equal amount of baking soda. Add a bit of water to make a paste.

Prepare the Headlight: Outline the headlight area with masking tape to avoid damaging the car's paint.

Apply the Paste: With a microfiber cloth, use the toothpaste and baking soda mix to wipe the headlight lens. Rub on to the surface in circular motions, paying extra attention to any oxidation or cloudiness.

Rinse and Dry: Rub for a few minutes, then rinse with water and dry with a clean cloth. The headlight is now ready to use.

Optional Steps:

Car Wax: Coat the headlight lens with car wax to shield it from future harm. This will also make it more shiny.

Polishing Compound: After the treatment, if the headlight is seriously oxidized or graying, you can apply a polishing compound. Use the compound as directed by the manufacturer and polish the headlight to restore its clarity.

Tips:

- First test the mixture on a small patch of the headlight to make sure the toothpaste and baking soda do not damage the light.

- Work in a well-ventilated area and don't get the mixture on the car's paint.

- Only if the headlight is badly damaged, or the method doesn't achieve good results, will professional restoration be required.

THIS DO-IT-YOURSELF headlamp cleaning kit, it is convenient and inexpensive to clear up headlight clarity and eliminate oxidation. This can be done with a few simple tools and ingredients, and is suitable for small-scale operation or simply domestic use.

Ingredients:

- White vinegar
- Baking soda
- Water
- Microfiber cloth or soft sponge

Tools Required:

- Mixing bowl
- Measuring spoons
- Soft cloth or sponge

Method to Prepare:

Create the Paste: Mix equal amounts of white vinegar and baking soda in a mixing bowl to make a paste. To start, add each of these in 1/4 cup amounts and adjust as necessary to get the consistency of paste.

Mix Thoroughly: Combine the ingredients thoroughly. The vinegar and baking soda will interact to produce a slight foam.

Application: With a soft cloth or sponge, apply the paste to the chrome surface. Massage the paste into the chrome, especially in spots that are tarnished or stained.

Scrub Gently: Scrubbing must be done slowly so as not to scratch the chrome surface.

Rinse and Dry: After you've scrubbed the chrome, be sure to rinse the surface right off with water, and then wipe it off with a clean cloth.

Usage:

USING EITHER A CLOTH or a sponge, rub the homemade chrome polish onto the chrome of your car, bike, or household appliances.

Additional Tips:

• Let the paste sit on the chrome for a few minutes to help remove stubborn stains or heavily tarnished areas.

• Do not use the same cloth for rinsing, so as not to smear on the paste again.

Caution:

• Smear the homemade chrome polish on a small, invisible section first to see that it doesn't damage or scratch.

• Don't use rough materials, or chemicals which might harm the chrome surface.

MAKING YOUR OWN CHROME polish is a more economical and environmentally friendly way of cleaning and restoring the shine to chrome surfaces. Commercialization requires reflection on market size, packaging, and distribution network for one's product. However, in order to meet quality and safety standards commercial sales may require testing and certification.

Rain Repellent for Windshields

Ingredients:

- Isopropyl alcohol (70% or higher)
- White vinegar
- Liquid dish soap (mild)

Tools Required:

- Spray bottle
- Funnel
- Mixing bowl

Method to Prepare:

Mixing Solution: Mix together in a mixing bowl 1 cup of isopropyl alcohol, 1 cup of water, 1 tablespoon of white vinegar, and 1 teaspoon of liquid dish soap. Then use a funnel to pour the mixture into a spray bottle.

Shake Well: Tightly close the spray bottle and shake it well until the ingredients are mixed thoroughly.

Usage:

WASH THE WINDSHIELD completely before application. apply this home-made rain repellent to a microfiber cloth and wipe over the windshield.

Using circular motions, wipe the windshield surface, taking care to cover the entire area.

Additional Tips:

- Take the rain repellent and apply it in a ventilated space.

● To work properly, the repellent must be reapplied every few weeks, or after washing the car.

Caution:

● Don't use this on hot windshields, or apply it in strong sunlight, where it evaporates too soon, and it's very hard to apply.

● First, be sure to test the solution on a small spot to determine whether it will damage or streak the windshield.

MAKING YOUR OWN WINDSHIELD rain repellent is the least expensive method to achieve better visibility in rain. This do-it-yourself formula can be readily made in batches and is therefore ideally suited to either small-scale production or use in the home.

Ingredients:

- Carnauba wax (flakes or solid form)
- Mineral spirits or naphtha
- Microfiber cloth or applicator pad

Tools Required:

- Double boiler or heat-safe container for melting wax
- Measuring cup
- Mixing spoon
- Airtight container for storage

Method to Prepare:

Melting the Wax: In a double boiler or a heat-safe container placed in a pot of simmering water, melt the carnauba wax. Use around 2 cups of carnauba wax flakes with 1 cup of mineral spirits or naphtha. Stir occasionally until the wax completely melts and combines with the solvent.

Cooling and Mixing: Let the mixture cool slightly. Stir it gently to ensure the wax and solvent are thoroughly combined.

Transfer to Container: Pour the mixture into an airtight container for storage. Allow it to cool and solidify before use.

Usage:

- Apply the paint sealant onto the car's clean and dry surface using a microfiber cloth or applicator pad. Use gentle circular motions to spread the sealant evenly.

- Allow the sealant to haze over (usually a few minutes) before buffing it off with a clean microfiber cloth.

Additional Tips:

- To prevent premature drying, apply the sealant in a shaded area.

- To protect more effectively, apply a number of thin layers of sealant. Each layer should be cured before you put on the next one.

- For future use, store the remaining sealant in a cool dry place.

Caution:

- Because mineral spirits or naphtha have fumes, work in a well-ventilated area.

- Do not allow these solvents to contact the eyes, and avoid prolonged skin exposure. If necessary, wear gloves and protective eyewear.

MAKING A DO-IT-YOURSELF paint sealant provides an inexpensive and effective method to preserve a car's exterior. Small-scale production or personal use This process print takes a bit more care, since solvents are used. But the whole thing can be done in very small quarters indeed.

Ingredients:

- Liquid Castile Soap (unscented): ½ cup

- Water: ½ cup

- Aloe Vera Gel: 2 tablespoons

- Coconut Oil: 1 tablespoon

- Essential Oil (optional, for fragrance): 5-10 drops of pet-safe essential oil (e.g., lavender, chamomile)

Tools and Equipment:

- Mixing bowl
- Clean and sterilized bottle for storage
- Stirring utensil (spoon or whisk)

Method:

Prepare Your Workspace: When making the pet shampoo, make sure your work area and your equipment are clean and sanitized.

Mixing the Ingredients: Combine the liquid castile soap, water, aloe vera gel and coconut oil in a mixing bowl. Stir with a spoon or whisk until thoroughly combined.

Optional Essential Oil: Add 5 to 10 drops of pet-friendly essential oil as fragrance, if using essential oil. Stir again to distribute the fragrance evenly.

Transfer to Storage Bottle: Pour the prepared pet shampoo into a clean, sterilized bottle, which can be stored. The bottle should have a tight-fitting lid so it doesn't spill.

Label and Store: write on the bottle the date of preparation, together with any necessary usage instructions. Keep the pet shampoo in a cool, dry place.

Additional Tips:

- Application: During bath time, use the homemade pet shampoo on your pet. Rub a little onto wet fur, lather, and rinse thoroughly.

- Skin Sensitivity: Before using this pet shampoo, perform a patch test (especially if your pet has sensitive skin or allergies to some ingredients).

- Shelf Life: If stored properly, the shampoo will last for several months.

THIS DO-IT-YOURSELF pet shampoo offers a natural, gentle alternative to washing your pet. It can be made in small quantities for personal use, or perhaps even as part of a small manufacturing factory. Always use high-quality ingredients and ensure they are suitable for your pet's skin and coat. Adjust the recipe according to your preferences and any sensitivities your pet might have.

Ingredients:

- Apple Cider Vinegar: ½ cup

- Water: ½ cup

- Coconut Oil: 1 tablespoon

- Aloe Vera Gel: 1 tablespoon

- Vegetable Glycerin: 1 teaspoon

- Lavender Essential Oil (optional, for fragrance): 5-10 drops of pet-safe essential oil

Tools and Equipment:

- Mixing bowl
- Clean and sterilized bottle for storage
- Stirring utensil (spoon or whisk)

Method:

Prepare Your Workspace: Be sure your work space and tools are clean and disinfected for making the pet polish.

Mixing the Ingredients: Combine the apple cider vinegar and water in a mixing bowl. Mix together gently with a spoon or whisk.

Add Oils and Glycerin: Mix the vinegar and water with the coconut oil, aloe vera gel and vegetable glycerin. Stir thoroughly so that the ingredients are completely mixed.

Optional Essential Oil: If essential oil is used for fragrance, add 5-10 drops of pet-safe essential oil to the mixture. Stir again to distribute the fragrance evenly.

Transfer to Storage Bottle: Gently pour the ready-made pet conditioner into a clean, sterilized storage bottle. The bottle needs a good-fitting tight lid so as not to spill.

Label and Store: Place the date of preparation and any necessary usage instructions on the bottle. Keep the pet conditioner in a cool, dry place.

Additional Tips:

• Application: After your pet has been shampooed, apply the homemade pet conditioner. Rub a little on your pet's clean, wet fur. Massage in, leave on for a few minutes, then rinse off thoroughly.

• Skin Sensitivity: Before using the pet conditioner, perform a patch test, especially if your pet's skin is sensitive, or if your pet is allergic to certain ingredients.

• Shelf Life: If stored properly, the conditioner will last for several months.

MADE AT HOME, THIS pet conditioner is environmentally friendly and nutritious. It can be made in smaller quantities, for private use or perhaps even as part of a small-scale production plant. Ensure the ingredients are always high-quality and are well-suited for your pet's skin and coat. Alter this recipe according to your taste and whatever allergies your animal has.

Ingredients:

- Distilled Water: 1 cup

- Apple Cider Vinegar: ½ cup

- Aloe Vera Gel: 2 tablespoons

- Vegetable Glycerin: 1 teaspoon

- Lavender Essential Oil (optional, for fragrance): 5-10 drops of pet-safe essential oil

Tools and Equipment:

- Mixing bowl
- Clean and sterilized spray bottle for storage
- Stirring utensil (spoon or whisk)

Method:

Prepare Your Workspace: When making the pet deodorizing spray, be sure to clean your work surface and instruments.

Mixing the Ingredients: Put the distilled water and apple cider vinegar in a mixing bowl. Stir the mixture gently with a spoon or whisk.

Add Aloe Vera and Glycerin: Add the aloe vera gel and vegetable glycerin to the water and vinegar. Stir thoroughly to get all the ingredients well mixed.

Optional Essential Oil: If you want to use essential oil as fragrance, add 5-10 drops of pet-safe essential oil to the mixture. Stir once more to spread the scent evenly.

Transfer to Storage Bottle: Pour the prepared pet deodorizing spray into a clean, sterilized spray bottle in which you can store it. Make sure the bottle has a spray nozzle and a closely-fitting lid to prevent dripping.

Label and Store: Write the date of preparation and any necessary usage instructions on the bottle. Keep the pet deodorizing spray in a cool, dry place.

Additional Tips:

● Application: Shake the bottle thoroughly before each use. Using homemade pet deodorizing spray, spray it onto your pet's coat, but do not contact the eyes and face. Either let him air dry or towel-dry him gently.

● Skin Sensitivity: Test for a patch before using the spray, especially if your pet is sensitive or allergic to some of the ingredients.

● Shelf Life: If stored properly, the spray can last several months.

THIS HOME-MADE PET-deodorizing spray provides a natural, refreshing alternative choice for keeping your animal smelling fragrant. It can be made in small batches for personal use, or even integrated into a small-scale production system. Keep your ingredients high-quality and select only those that are suitable for your pet's skin. Adapt the recipe to suit your taste and your pet's sensibilities.

Ingredients:

- Coconut Oil: 2 tablespoons

- Shea Butter: 2 tablespoons

- Beeswax: 1 tablespoon

- Sweet Almond Oil or Olive Oil: 1 tablespoon

- Vitamin E Oil: ½ teaspoon

- Lavender Essential Oil (optional, for fragrance): 5-10 drops of pet-safe essential oil

Tools and Equipment:

- Double boiler or heat-safe bowl and saucepan
- Mixing bowl
- Clean and sterilized container or tin for storage
- Stirring utensil (spoon or spatula)

Method:

Prepare Your Workspace: When making pet paw balm, be sure your work surface and your tools are clean and germ-free.

Melt Ingredients: Place the bowl over a saucepan of simmering water. Alternatively, use a double boiler. Add the coconut oil, shea butter, beeswax, and sweet almond oil or olive oil to the bowl. Just allow them to melt, stirring occasionally with a spoon or spatula until fully melted and combined.

Incorporate Vitamin E Oil: After melting, remove the mixture from heat. Pour the vitamin E oil into the melted mixture. Stir well until it is well mixed.

Optional Essential Oil: If using essential oil for fragrance, add 5-10 drops of pet-safe essential oil to the mixture.

Stir again to distribute the fragrance evenly.

Transfer to Storage Container: Carefully pour the prepared pet paw balm into a clean and sterilized container or tin suitable for storage. Ensure the container has a tight-fitting lid.

Cool and Set: Let the balm cool and set at room temperature for a few hours or until it solidifies.

Label and Store: Label the container with the date of preparation and any necessary usage instructions. Store the pet paw balm in a cool, dry place away from direct sunlight.

Additional Tips:

- Application: Rub a little dab of the home-made pet paw balm onto your pet's paw pads, massaging gently to moisturize and prevent dryness or cracking.

- Skin Sensitivity: Before using the paw balm, do a skin test on your pet. Your pet's skin may be sensitive or allergic to some ingredients, so take care.

- Shelf Life: If stored properly, the balm will last for several months.

THIS HOMEMADE ANIMAL paw balm is a natural and protective application for your pet's paw pads. It can be made in small quantities for personal use, and even as part of a small-scale production site. Be sure the ingredients are of high quality and suitable for the skin of your dog. Adapt the recipe to meet your own tastes, and especially any allergies your pet may have.

Doggie Dry Shampoo

Ingredients:

- Cornstarch: ½ cup

- Baking Soda: ½ cup

- Oat Flour or Ground Oats: 2 tablespoons

- Lavender Essential Oil (optional, for fragrance): 5-10 drops of pet-safe essential oil

Tools and Equipment:

- Mixing bowl
- Clean and sterilized container for storage
- Applicator (such as a shaker bottle or powder dispenser)
- Brush or comb (optional)

Method:

Prepare Your Workspace: When making the doggie dry shampoo, make sure your workspace and tools are clean and sanitized.

Mixing the Ingredients: In a mixing bowl, mix the cornstarch, baking soda and oat flour or ground oats. Make sure the ingredients are well combined by thorough stirring.

Optional Essential Oil: Using essential oil as fragrance Add 5-10 drops of pet-safe essential oil to the dry mixture there. Stir again to mix the fragrance evenly.

Transfer to Storage Container: Pour the mixed doggie dry shampoo into a container that is clean and sterilized and suitable for storage. For application, an applicator like a shaker bottle or powder dispenser is ideal. Make sure the container fits with a tight-fitting lid.

Label and Store: Place instructions on the container, including the date of preparation, and any specifications for use. store the doggie dry shampoo in a cool, dry place away from humidity.

Additional Tips:

● Application: Sprinkle a small amount of the dry shampoo onto your dog's coat, especially on areas where the fur tends to get oily or dirty. Gently rub or brush the powder into the fur, then brush or comb out the excess.

● Avoid Eyes and Face: Make sure not to let the dry shampoo come near your dog's eyes or face.

● Shelf Life: Properly stored, the dry shampoo can last several months.

THIS SIMPLE DOGGIE dry shampoo provides a natural and hassle-free way to keep your dog's coat fresh between baths. It can be produced in small quantities for personal use or even as part of a small production setup. Only use the best ingredients, and make sure they match your pet's skin. Modify the recipe to suit your taste and any allergies your dog might have.

Ingredients:

- Fabric (cotton, fleece, or other cat-safe fabric): Scraps or pieces for toy shapes

- Catnip: Dried catnip herb or catnip pellets

- Stuffing material: Polyester fiberfill or organic cotton batting

Tools and Equipment:

- Sewing machine or needle and thread
- Scissors
- Pins
- Catnip-safe container for storage

Method:

Prepare Your Workspace: Prepare a clean work area and clear space to make catnip toys.

Cutting Shapes: Cut the fabric pieces into shapes suitable for cat toys. Square, rectangle, circles, even animal shapes, such as mice or fish, are common. Sizes should be kept small to medium for convenience in handling.

Sewing the Toy: Place two pieces of fabric together (inside out) for each toy. Precisely stick the parts together to keep them stable. Push the toy through a tiny opening.

Stuffing and Catnip: Add enough catnip to all the toys. Use dried catnip herb or catnip pellets instead. So that it is soft and pliant to the touch, stuff some stuffing material into the toy with the catnip.

Complete Sewing: Stuff the toy with catnip and stuffing, then sew shut the opening securely. Stitch or reinforce the ends, otherwise the catnip will stick out.

Trim and Finalize: Trim away any excess fabric and threads. Be sure that the toy is safe, and that no loose ends come undone.

Storage: Once a catnip toy is finished, put it in a catnip-resistant container, or seal it in a bag to retain its freshness.

Additional Tips:

- Fabric Selection: Choose tough fabrics that can withstand chewing and scratching.

- Catnip Amount: The right amount of catnip. For others, perhaps, too much is overwhelming, while too little fails to interest.

- Supervision: Catnip toys are ideal to keep a close eye on a cat, if your pet is a bad toy destroyer.

MAKING THIS HOMEMADE catnip toy is a good way to unleash your creativity. Vary the shape and size according to your taste. When shopping for materials, make sure they are safe for cats, and examine the toys from time to time to make sure they aren't old.

Ingredients:

- Protein Base: Choose protein sources such as fish fillets, shrimp, or worms (ensure they are safe for your fish and free from additives or seasonings)

- Vegetables: Options like spinach, peas, or zucchini can provide vitamins and fiber

- Gelatin or Agar Powder (optional): Helps bind the ingredients together

- Fish Oil (optional): Provides essential fatty acids

Tools and Equipment:

- Blender or food processor
- Ice cube trays or molds
- Plastic wrap or freezer bags for storage

Method:

Prepare Ingredients: Cook the chosen protein (fish, shrimp, worms) and vegetables well. They must be fully cooked and seasoning- and additive-free.

Blend Ingredients: Cut the cooked protein and vegetables into smaller pieces so you can blend them up more easily. In a blender or food processor, puree the cooked ingredients until they form a smooth paste. For additional nutrients, add fish oil, if desired.

Optional Binding Agent: If you want the fish food to keep its shape better, dissolve a little bit of gelatin or agar powder in water as directed on the package. Pour this into the blended mixture and stir thoroughly.

Mold and Freeze: Spoon the mixture into ice cube trays or molds. Flatten the mixture evenly. Wrap the trays in plastic wrap and put them in the freezer until the mixture sets.

Storage: Once hard, remove the fish food from the molds and place them in freezer bags or airtight containers. Store in the freezer until required.

Additional Tips:

- Fish Size and Diet: Adjust the ingredients and consistency to match the fish species 'specific dietary requirements.

- Variety: You can try out different ingredients to make different kinds of fish food,suitable for different kinds of fish.

ANOTHER ADVANTAGE OF home-made fish food is that you can dictate exactly what your fish should eat. Always do your homework and be sure that the ingredients you use for your particular fish are safe and suitable. You may want to consult with a veterinarian or expert for more exact dietary prescriptions for your fish. Alter the recipe according to your fish's dietary needs and tastes.

Ingredients:

- Paper Products: Newspaper, plain paper, or cardboard
- Hay or Straw (optional): For added comfort and nesting material
- Baking Soda (optional): To control odor

Tools and Equipment:

- Shredder or scissors
- Large container or bin
- Optional: Essential oils (pet-safe) for fragrance

Method:

Prepare Paper Products: Cut up newspaper, plain paper or cardboard into little strips or pieces. Verify that these materials do not possess ink, dyes, or other hazardous chemicals.

Optional Additions: If using hay or straw, then cut into smaller pieces and add to the shredded paper. Some baking soda added can help neutralize odors.

Mixing: In a large container or bin, mix together the shredded paper, the hay or straw if desired, and the baking soda. Mix them together really well to get a uniform mixture.

Optional Fragrance: If desired, add a few rose water drops or drops of some pet-safe essential oils to give it a fragrance. But be sure your pet can withstand these fragrances, since some animals may be sensitive to strong smells.

Storage: Place the homemade small animal bedding in a clean, dry container and bag until needed.

Additional Tips:

- Materials Selection: All the materials used must be safe and non-toxic for your small animal in particular. Do not use materials that contain ink, chemicals, or synthetic perfumes.

- Monitoring Pets: If your pets' new bedding caused any allergic reaction or discomfort, observe them. Check for any itching or allergic reaction.

HOME-MADE LITTLE ANIMAL bedding is economical as well as customizable. Always think of the safety and comfort of your pets when producing bedding materials. Based on the actual needs and sensitivities of your small animals, you must adjust the recipe and materials.

Ingredients and Materials:

- Soy Wax Flakes or Beeswax - Quantity depends on the size of the jar(s)

- Candle Wicks - Pre-tabbed with a metal base, sized for your jar(s)

- Mason Jars - Clean and dry, in the desired size

- Fragrance Oil or Essential Oil - Optional, for scent (approximately 1 ounce per pound of wax)

- Candle Dye or Coloring (if desired) - Optional, for color

- Double Boiler or Heat Proof Container and Saucepan

- Stirring Utensil (Metal Spoon or Stir Stick)

- Thermometer

- Wick Holder or Pencil and Tape

Method:

Prepare the Jars and Wicks:

Place the wick in the center of the mason jar. Use a wick holder or tie the top of the wick around a pencil placed across the jar's opening. Ensure the wick stays centered and straight.

Melt the Wax:

Use a double boiler or a heat proof container placed in a saucepan with water. Place the soy wax flakes or beeswax in the container and melt them over medium heat. Monitor the temperature using a thermometer.

Adding Fragrance and Color (if using):

When the wax is melted and reaches about 180-185°F (82-85°C), add the fragrance oil or essential oil. Add coloring at this point if using coloring. Stir gently to combine thoroughly.

Pouring the Wax:

Pour the melted wax into the prepared jars, making sure that the wick still remains centered. Allow for half an inch to an inch space at the top of the jar.

Setting the Wick:

Allow the candles to rest for several hours until the wax hardens. If necessary, you can use a pencil or stick to straighten out the wick while the wax remains soft.

Trimming the Wick:

After the wax has completely cooled and solidified, cut the wick to 1/4 inch above the surface of the candle.

Curing Time:

Allow the candles to cure for at least 24-48 hours after pouring so fragrance can completely blend with the wax.

Additional Tips:

- Safety First: Do your work in a well-ventilated area and be careful when handling hot wax.

- Experiment: You are welcome to substitute different scents, colors, and sizes of mason jars to produce different styles of candles.

MASON JAR CANDLES CAN be a lovely addition to your home, or a nice gift. Always exercise caution when working with hot wax and follow safety guidelines for candle making. Adjust the quantities of fragrance oil and coloring based on personal preferences for scent strength and color intensity.

Ingredients and Materials:

- Beeswax Sheets or Beeswax Pellets: Approximately 1 pound (for several candles)

- Candle Wick: Pre-waxed wicks work well

- Optional: Essential oils for fragrance (if desired)

Tools:

- Double boiler or a heat proof container and saucepan for melting wax
- Stirring utensil (wooden stick or spoon)
- Scissors
- Wick holder or pencil

Method:

Prepare the Wick: Measure and cut the wick to the desired length, allowing a few extra inches for the wick to stand above the candle. Attach the wick to a wick holder or wrap it around a pencil to keep it centered while pouring the wax.

Melting the Beeswax: If using beeswax sheets, cut them into manageable sizes for melting. To make a makeshift double boiler, use a double boiler, or a heatproof container set in a saucepan of water a few inches deep. In the top container melt the beeswax over medium heat, until it melts completely. But using pellets, just melt them straight in the double boiler.

Adding Fragrance (Optional): If you prefer, add a few drops of essential oil to the melted beeswax and stir in gently until the scent is evenly distributed.

Pouring the Wax: Slowly pour the melted beeswax into a heat resistant candle mold or container. If using a container, keep the wick centered as you pour. Hold the wick steady until the wax cools slightly, keeping it centered.

Setting and Trimming: Let the wax cool and harden completely. After hardening, cut the wick to a length about 1/4 inch above the surface of the wax.

Finishing: Optionally, you may decorate the candle by wrapping a ribbon around the base or by adding decorative elements before the wax has fully hardened.

Safety Note: Melt beeswax carefully every time and never leave it heating unattended. Take care to avoid burns or fires.

Tips:

- Mold the wax into different shapes by using different molds or containers.

- Natural honey scent: Beeswax candles are heavenly scented. But if you want a stronger scent, you can enhance it with essential oils, or leave it unscented.

- Stabilize a surface for the candles to cool and harden evenly.

THESE HANDMADE BEESWAX candles bring a warm and comfortable atmosphere to anywhere. Take safety precautions and have fun in the process of making these fun candles.

Ingredients:

- Olive Oil - 1/4 cup
- White Vinegar - 3/4 cup
- Essential Oils - 10-15 drops (optional, for fragrance and added shine)

Equipment/Tools:

- Mixing bowl or container
- Spray bottle or airtight container
- Soft cloth for polishing

Method:

Prepare Your Workspace:
Make sure your work area is clean and dry. Collect all the ingredients and tools you need.

Mix the Ingredients:

Combine the olive oil and white vinegar in a mixing bowl or container. Stir or whisk the mixture well to combine the ingredients.

Optional: Add Essential Oils:

If preferred, add 10-15 drops of essential oils to the mixture for scent and extra shine. Lemon or orange oil add a beautiful fragrance to furniture polish.

Transfer to a Container:

Pour the homemade furniture polish into a spray bottle or an airtight container for storage.

Label and Store:

Label the container with description and date of preparation. Store it in a dry & cool place, avoid direct sunlight.

How to Use:

● Shake the container well before using, ensure the ingredients are mixed.

● Spray a small amount of the polish onto a soft cloth.

● Gently polish the furniture with the cloth, using circular motions to apply the polish evenly. Be sure to cover the entire surface.

Additional Tips:

● Usage: Use this homemade furniture polish to clean and shine wood furniture. It helps in nourishing and giving a natural shine to the wood.

● Adjustments: You can adjust the quantity of essential oils for a preferred scent or skip them altogether.

THIS DIY FURNITURE polish offers a natural and effective way to clean and polish wood furniture. Always perform a patch test in an inconspicuous area to ensure compatibility with your furniture. Adjust the ingredients according to your preferences.

Ingredients:

Olive Oil - 1/4 cup

White Vinegar - 1/4 cup

Lemon Essential Oil - 10-15 drops (optional, for fragrance and added cleaning properties)

Equipment/Tools:

- Mixing bowl or container
- Soft cloth or microfiber towel

Method:

Prepare Your Workspace:
Make sure your work area is clean and dry. Gather together all the necessary ingredients and utensils.

Mix the Ingredients:
Combine the olive oil and white vinegar in a mixing bowl or container. Stir or shake the mixture well to combine the ingredients.

Optional: Add Essential Oil:
If you like, add 10-15 drops of lemon essential oil to the mixture for an attractive fragrance and additional cleaning ability. Citrus oils like lemon or orange are effective.

Apply the Wood Polish:
Dip a soft cloth or microfiber towel into the homemade wood polish.

Using a circular motion, apply the polish onto the wood surface, to ensure thorough and even coating.

Buffing:
Let the polish rest on the wood for a few minutes.

Use a clean, dry cloth and rub the wood surface in the direction of the grain. Buff the surface until it looks shiny.

Additional Tips:

- Usage: Pour this wood polish onto wooden furniture, cabinets, or other wooden surfaces to rub clean and lustrous.

- Adjustments: You may add as much essential oil as you need to scent the wood, or leave out the essential oil altogether.

NATURAL AND EFFECTIVE This DIY wood polish nourishes and brings a shine to wooden surfaces. Always test the polish in a small, inconspicuous area first to determine whether or not it is compatible with the wood type. Adjust the ingredients to suit your own taste and the needs of your wooden pieces.

Ingredients:

Steel Wool - 1 pad (for aging effect)
White Vinegar - 1 cup
Coffee Grounds - 1/4 cup
Boiling Water - 1 cup
Black Tea Bags - 2-3 bags (for a darker stain)
Mason Jar or Container with Lid

Equipment/Tools:

- Mason jar or container for mixing and storage
- Fine-mesh strainer or cheesecloth
- Paintbrush or cloth for application
- Gloves (optional, for protection)

Method:

Prepare the Steel Wool Solution:

Place a steel wool pad in a mason jar or container and pour in the white vinegar. Seal the jar with a lid and let it sit for at least 24 hours or until the steel wool completely dissolves. This will create an aging effect for the wood.

Prepare the Coffee and Tea Solution:

MAKE STRONG COFFEE with the coffee grounds and boiling water. While the coffee is still hot, steep the black tea bags in the coffee. Allow the mixture to cool.

Combine Solutions:

When the steel wool has dissolved in the vinegar, strain the liquid using a fine-mesh strainer or cheesecloth to remove any remaining particles.

Combine the cold coffee and tea with the strained steel wool solution. Adjust the quantities to achieve the desired intensity of color.

Application:

Before applying the home-made wood stain, the surface of the wood needs to be clean and dry.

Apply the stain to the wood surface with a paintbrush or cloth. Rub in the direction of the wood's grain, covering evenly.

Allow the stain to soak into the wood for a few minutes. If you want a darker color, apply another coat as required, allowing the color to dry between coats.

Finish:

Once you have gotten the desired color, let the stain dry completely.

Apply a coat of clear sealant or varnish to protect the stained wood surface.

Additional Tips:

- Usage: This homemade wood stain gives wood a natural tint and provides an aged effect. Test the stain on a small area first to get the color you want.

- Adjustments: Vary the amounts of ingredients to get the right color. Different color tones can be achieved by varying the strength of the coffee and tea.

NATURAL WOOD STAINS are homemade stains that can color wood surfaces. Take your wood staining project's special needs and tastes into account and adjust the ingredients and application process accordingly.

Ingredients:

Beeswax - 1/2 cup
Mineral Oil - 1/2 cup
Carnauba Wax - 1 tablespoon (optional, for added protection)
Essential Oil (Optional, for fragrance)

Equipment/Tools:

- Double boiler or makeshift one (a pot and heat-resistant container)
- Stirring utensil (metal spoon or wooden stick)
- Container for storage

Method:

Prepare Your Workspace:
Ensure your workspace is clean and dry. Gather the tools and ingredients needed.

Melt the Ingredients:

USE A DOUBLE BOILER (or a pot with a heat-resistant container inside) to melt the beeswax and mineral oil together over low to medium heat. Stir occasionally until the mixture is fully melted and combined.

Optional: Add Carnauba Wax and Essential Oil:

OPTIONALLY, ADD CARNAUBA wax to the melted blend for extra protection. Stir until it melts and combines.

Add a few drops of essential oil for a fragrance. Oils like cedarwood or tea tree may add a pleasant perfume.

Transfer to Storage Container:

Pour the melted wood preservative mixture into a suitable container, carefully. Let it cool and solidify.

How to Use:

WITH A CLEAN CLOTH or brush, spread the wood preservative over clean, dry wood surfaces.

Allow the preservative to penetrate the wood grain.

Let the wood soak up the preservative, and wipe it off after a few minutes.

Should another coat be needed, repeat the application process, waiting for each layer to dry before applying the next.

Additional Tips:

● Usage: This homemade wood preservative protects and conditions the wood and makes it resistant to moisture and decay.

● Adjustments: The proportions can also be adjusted. The greater the number of beeswax and the lesser the amount of mineral oil, the thicker the consistency.

● Always perform a trial application of the homemade wood preservative on a small section of the wood in order to make sure it offers the desired level of protection and appearance. Adjust the ingredients to your taste and the particular needs of the wood you're treating.

Tile and Grout cleaner

Ingredients:

- Baking Soda - 1/2 cup
- Hydrogen Peroxide - 1/4 cup
- Liquid Dish Soap - 1 teaspoon
- Water - Enough to make a paste
- Vinegar - Optional, for added cleaning power and disinfection

Equipment/Tools:

- Mixing bowl or container
- Soft-bristled brush or toothbrush
- Spray bottle (if using vinegar)

Method:

Prepare Your Workspace:
Ventilate your work space properly. Gather all the ingredients and tools.

Mix the Ingredients:

Combine the baking soda, hydrogen peroxide, liquid dish soap and a little water in a mixing bowl or container. Stir thoroughly, until you have a thick, spreadable paste.

Application:

Spread paste onto grout lines and tile surfaces with a soft-bristled brush or toothbrush. Make sure the paste has completely covered the areas you want to clean.

Scrubbing:

With the brush, scrub the paste into the grout lines and tile surfaces. Pay attention to any stained or discolored spots.

Optional: Vinegar Rinse (for extra cleaning):

To make the cleaning stronger, spray vinegar directly on the paste-covered areas. The vinegar will react with the baking soda, generating a foaming effect that helps clean and disinfect. Allow it to stand for a few minutes.

Rinsing:

Rinse the tile and grout thoroughly with water after scrubbing. Wipe away any residue with a clean, damp cloth.

Drying:

After cleaning the surfaces allow them to air dry or wipe them with a clean dry cloth.

Additional Tips:

- Usage: This home-made cleaner is effective against tile and grout in bathrooms, kitchens or wherever there is tile.

- Adjustments: According to the amount you need to clean, you can adjust the quantities to make more or less paste.

BEFORE USING HOMEMADE tile and grout cleaner for the first time, always test on a small, hidden area. Otherwise the cleaner may cause damage or discoloration. Adapt the ingredients and scrubbing degree in accordance with the level of cleaning required for your own tiles and grout.

Simple Alcohol-Based Perfume

Ingredients:

Essential Oils - A blend of your choice (for example):
- Lavender Essential Oil - 10 drops
- Bergamot Essential Oil - 5 drops
- Patchouli Essential Oil - 3 drops

Witch Hazel - 1 tablespoon (acts as a fixative)
Distilled Water - 2 tablespoons (for dilution)
Dark-Colored Glass Perfume Bottle with a spray or rollerball applicator

Equipment/Tools:

- Glass droppers for measuring essential oils
- Mixing bowl or beaker
- Funnel (optional)
- Small whisk or stirrer

Method:

Prepare Your Workspace:
Keep the workplace clean and dry. Collect all the ingredients and tools required.

Blend Essential Oils:

Place all your chosen essential oils together in a mixing bowl or beaker. Play around with different combinations and adjust the number of drops until you get the scent you desire.

Add Witch Hazel:

Then add the witch hazel to the essential oil blend. It works as a fixative, making the fragrance last longer.

Dilute with Distilled Water:

While stirring continuously, add the distilled water slowly. This weakens the fragrance and makes it less strong.

Mix Thoroughly:

Stir together all ingredients thoroughly with a small whisk or stirrer. Make sure all parts are well integrated.

Transfer to Perfume Bottle:

If necessary, use a funnel to pour the perfume mixture into a dark-colored glass perfume bottle with a spray or rollerball applicator.

Label and Store:

Write the date and the type of perfume on the bottle. Store in a cool and dry place, protected from direct sunlight.

Additional Tips:

- Fragrance Strength: Test the perfume by spraying or applying a small amount on your skin to gauge the strength of the fragrance. Adjust the essential oil ratios accordingly.

- Maturity of Fragrance: Allow the perfume to "age" for a few days or up to a week for the scents to blend and mature before regular use.

THIS DIY PERFUME ALLOWS you to create a personalized fragrance tailored to your preferences. Experiment with different essential oil blends and adjust the proportions to achieve your desired scent profile.

Ingredients:

Distilled Water - 2 ounces (about 1/4 cup)
Witch Hazel - 1 ounce (about 2 tablespoons)
Essential Oils - A blend of your choice (for example):
- Lavender Essential Oil - 10 drops
- Lemon Essential Oil - 5 drops
- Peppermint Essential Oil - 5 drops
Dark-Colored Glass Spray Bottle

Equipment/Tools:

- Glass droppers for measuring essential oils
- Mixing bowl or beaker
- Funnel (optional)

Method:

Prepare Your Workspace:
You need to keep your working area clean and dry. Assemble all the ingredients and tools required.

Blend Essential Oils:

Place your chosen essential oils in a mixing bowl or beaker. So go ahead, try different combinations and vary the number of drops to fashion your own room fragrance.

Combine with Witch Hazel:

Now add the witch hazel to the essential oil blend. This emulsifies the oils and allows them to mix with the water evenly.

Add Distilled Water:

While continuously stirring, gradually pour the distilled water into the mixture. It thins down the essential oils, and is the foundation for the room spray.

Mix Thoroughly:

Stir the mixture well to ensure the essential oils are completely combined with the water and alcohol.

Transfer to Spray Bottle:

If necessary, use a funnel to slowly pour the room spray mixture into a dark-colored glass spray bottle.

Shake Before Use:

Before you use the room spray, gently shake the bottle to mix the ingredients.

Label and Store:

Write the date and type of room spray on the bottle. Store in a cool, dry place away from direct sunlight.

Additional Tips:

● Scent Strength: Spray a small amount in the air to test the strength of the fragrance of the room spray. If necessary, adjust the proportions of the essential oils.

● Refreshing Effect: Mist lightly over living spaces, linens or upholstery to freshen up with room spray.

THIS HOMEMADE ROOM spray is an excellent way to create a natural and personalized scent for the home. Mix and match different essential oils, and adjust the proportions, to create different scents.

Ingredients:

Baking Soda - 1/2 cup
Essential Oils - A blend of your choice (for example):
- Tea Tree Essential Oil - 10 drops
- Lemon Essential Oil - 10 drops
- Eucalyptus Essential Oil - 5 drops
Small Mason Jar or Container with a Lid

Equipment/Tools:

- Mixing bowl
- Spoon or whisk for mixing

Method:

Prepare Your Workspace:

- Ensure your workspace is clean and dry. Gather the tools and ingredients needed.

Combine Baking Soda and Essential Oils:

- In a mixing bowl, add the baking soda.

- Carefully drop the essential oils onto the baking soda. This will help distribute the fragrance.

Mix Thoroughly:

- Use a spoon or whisk to mix the essential oils into the baking soda thoroughly. Ensure that the oils are evenly distributed throughout the baking soda.

Transfer to Container:

- Carefully spoon the scented baking soda mixture into a small mason jar or any airtight container with a lid.

Close and Store:

- Seal the container with the lid tightly to preserve the scent.

Additional Tips:

- Scent Intensity: Adjust the number of drops of essential oils to achieve the desired strength of fragrance.

- Usage: Place the air freshener in areas such as closets, drawers, bathrooms, or any space needing a fresh scent. Shake or stir occasionally to release the scent.

This DIY air freshener is a simple and effective way to naturally freshen up different areas in your home. The baking soda helps absorb odors, while the essential oils provide a pleasant scent. Feel free to experiment with different essential oil combinations to create your preferred fragrance.

Ingredients:

Carrier Oil (optional, for dilution) - Jojoba oil, sweet almond oil, or fractionated coconut oil

Essential Oils - A blend of your choice (for example):

- Lavender Essential Oil - 10 drops

- Peppermint Essential Oil - 5 drops

- Eucalyptus Essential Oil - 5 drops

Equipment/Tools:

- Glass droppers for measuring essential oils
- Mixing bottle or small glass container
- Stirring utensil (stir stick or glass dropper)

Method:

Prepare Your Workspace:
Make sure your work area is clean and dry. Collect the materials and ingredients.

Choose Essential Oils:

Choose the essential oils that you want to combine according their aromatherapy applications and your own tastes.

Measure Essential Oils:

With the help of glass droppers, place the measured drops of each essential oil into the mixing bottle or glass container.

Optional Dilution with Carrier Oil:

If you prefer a weaker blend, top off the remainder of the container with a carrier oil, allowing space for the oils to permeate when shaken. This step is optional, and can be omitted if you prefer the blend undiluted.

Mix Thoroughly:

Seal up the container and shake it gently, or use a stir stick to mix the essential oils. See that the oils are well combined.

Label and Store:

On the outside of the container write the blend's name and the date. Store in a cool, dry place away from direct sunlight.

Additional Tips:

- Blending Ratios: Experiment with different ratios of essential oils to make unique scents and to create therapeutic effects.

- Usage: To use, blend in a diffuser, as a room spray, in a bath, or diluted with a carrier oil for topical application, having first performed a patch test.

WITH HOMEMADE ESSENTIAL oil blends, you can pick and choose the scents you like, and take advantage of the possible therapeutic effects of different oils. Balance the blend after your own taste and with your desired effects in mind (note: Follow safety guidelines and recommended dilution ratios for topical use).

Ingredients and Materials:

Wooden Sticks or Bamboo Skewers - for the base
Wood Powder or Sawdust - 1 cup
Makko Powder or Gum Arabic - 1/4 cup (natural binder)
Essential Oils or Fragrance Oils - 20-30 drops (for scent)
Water - 1-2 tablespoons
Mortar and Pestle or Grinder (if needed to crush herbs)
Small Bowl or Container for Mixing

Method:

Prepare the Base:

If you use wooden sticks, they must be clean and dry. If using bamboo skewers, cut away any sharp points and cut them to the length desired.

Prepare the Mixture:

Wood powder or sawdust in a small bowl or container Mix the makko powder or gum Arabic into it. This becomes the foundation of the incense.

Add Fragrance:

Pour your selected essential oils or fragrance oils on the dry mixture. With a dropper, divide the scent evenly through the powder. Thoroughly mixed to ensure equal distribution of scent.

Add Water:

Add water a little at a time, gradually mixing the dry ingredients together. The consistency you want is dough-like: When pressed, it should hold together but not be too wet.

Forming the Sticks:

Take a little of the incense mixture and roll it between your palms into sticks or cones. If using wooden sticks or bamboo skewers, simply spoon a bit of the mixture onto the sticks, leaving some 2/3 of their length uncovered.

Drying:

Dispense the incense sticks or cones onto a flat surface spread out with parchment paper or a non-stick mat. Let them dry naturally in a cool, dry place for 24-48 hours. It makes the incense harden and dry out completely.

Curing:

Dry the sticks or cones. Cure them in a well-ventilated place for a few days. This helps the scents to ripen and become more full-bodied in scent.

Usage Tips:

● Burning: Light the tip of the incense stick or cone. Allow the flame to burn for a few seconds and then blow it out. It should smolder and exude fragrance.

● Storage: The incense sticks or cones should be stored in an airtight container in a cool, dry place until use.

Ingredients and Materials:

Glass Container or Vase - for holding the diffuser liquid

Diffuser Base Oil - 4 ounces (such as a carrier oil like fractionated coconut oil or mineral oil)

Essential Oils - Around 20-30 drops (for fragrance)

Reed Diffuser Sticks - Several reeds for diffusion (number varies based on container size)

Rubbing Alcohol - Optional, for thinning the oil mixture (1-2 tablespoons)

Funnel - for pouring liquids into the container

Method:

Prepare the Container:
      Clean and dry the glass container or vase that will hold the diffuser liquid. Ensure it's free of any dust or residue.

Mix the Diffuser Base:

IN A SEPARATE CONTAINER, combine the diffuser base oil with your chosen essential oils. Stir or gently shake the mixture to blend the oils thoroughly.

Optional: Thin the Mixture:

IF THE OIL BLEND IS too thick, you can add 1-2 tablespoons of rubbing alcohol to thin the mixture. This helps the oil travel up the reeds more easily.

Pour the Mixture into the Container:

USE A FUNNEL TO POUR the oil mixture into the glass container or vase. Fill it to about 3/4 full, leaving room at the top for the reeds and diffusion.

Add the Reeds:

INSERT THE REED DIFFUSER sticks into the container with the oil mixture. Let them soak for a couple of hours or overnight to absorb the oils.

Flip the Reeds:

AFTER A FEW HOURS OR overnight, flip the reeds so that the saturated ends are now at the top. This helps refresh the diffusion.

Place and Enjoy:

PLACE THE REED DIFFUSER in your desired location, ideally in a spot with good airflow. The essential oils will gradually diffuse into the air through the reeds, providing a subtle, continuous fragrance.

Usage Tips:

- Rotation: For a stronger scent, you can rotate the reeds every few days.

- Adjustments: Alter the number of reeds used or the essential oil combinations to achieve the desired fragrance strength.

REED DIFFUSERS OFFER a convenient and subtle way to add fragrance to your space without the need for heat or electricity. Experiment with different essential oil blends to create scents that suit your preferences and mood.

Ingredients for Stick Deodorant:

Coconut Oil - 3 tablespoons
Shea Butter - 2 tablespoons
Beeswax - 2 tablespoons
Baking Soda - 3 tablespoons
Arrowroot Powder or Cornstarch - 3 tablespoons
Essential Oils - 15-20 drops (for fragrance, optional)

Ingredients for Cream Deodorant:

Coconut Oil - 1/4 cup
Shea Butter - 2 tablespoons
Arrowroot Powder or Cornstarch - 1/4 cup
Baking Soda - 2 tablespoons
Essential Oils - 15-20 drops (for fragrance, optional)

Equipment/Tools:

- Double boiler or makeshift one (a pot and heat-resistant container)
- Mixing bowl
- Spoon or spatula
- Deodorant container (for stick) or jar (for cream)

Method:

Melt Ingredients:

- Use a double boiler (or a pot with a heat-resistant container inside) to melt the coconut oil, shea butter, and beeswax together over low heat.

Add Dry Ingredients:

● Once melted, remove the mixture from heat. Add the baking soda and arrowroot powder (or cornstarch) to the melted oils. Mix well until a smooth consistency is achieved.

Add Essential Oils:

● If using essential oils for fragrance, add them to the mixture. Stir thoroughly to evenly distribute the oils.

Pour into Container:

● For stick deodorant: Pour the mixture into a deodorant container while it's still liquid. Allow it to cool and solidify.

● For cream deodorant: Pour the mixture into a clean jar or container suitable for storage. It will solidify as it cools.

Usage:

● For stick deodorant: Apply as you would with a commercial stick deodorant, swiping it onto clean, dry underarms.

● For cream deodorant: Use a small amount and apply it to clean, dry underarms with your fingers.

Usage Tips:

● Test Patch: Always perform a patch test on a small area of your skin to ensure you don't have any adverse reactions to the ingredients.

● Consistency: If you prefer a softer or firmer deodorant, adjust the amounts of ingredients accordingly in future batches.

Homemade deodorants provide a natural alternative to commercial products. Adjust the amount of baking soda if you have sensitive skin, as some individuals may be sensitive to it. Store the deodorant in a cool, dry place for use.

Ingredients:

- Beeswax: 1 tablespoon

- Jojoba Oil or Sweet Almond Oil: 1 tablespoon

- Essential Oils (or fragrance oils) of your choice: 20-25 drops (total combined)

Tools and Equipment:

- Double boiler or heat-safe bowl and saucepan
- Small containers or tins for storing the solid perfume
- Stirring utensil (spatula or small spoon)

Method:

Prepare Your Workspace: Ensure your workspace and tools are clean and sanitized for making the solid perfume.

Melt Beeswax and Oil: Use a double boiler or a heat-safe bowl placed over a saucepan with simmering water. Add the beeswax and jojoba oil or sweet almond oil to the bowl. Allow them to melt gently, stirring occasionally with a spoon or spatula until fully melted and combined.

Add Essential Oils: Once melted, remove the mixture from heat. Add your chosen essential oils or fragrance oils to the melted wax and oil mixture. Stir well to evenly distribute the scent.

Transfer to Containers: Carefully pour the perfume mixture into clean and sterilized small containers or tins suitable for storing solid perfume. Ensure the containers are airtight.

Cool and Set: Allow the perfume to cool and set at room temperature for a few hours or until completely solidified.

Label and Store: Label the containers with the date of preparation and the names of the scents used. Store the solid perfume in a cool, dry place away from direct sunlight.

Additional Tips:

- Application: To use the solid perfume, simply rub a small amount onto pulse points such as wrists, behind the ears, or at the base of the throat.

- Scent Combinations: Experiment with different essential oil blends to create your desired fragrance. Popular combinations include lavender and vanilla, citrus and bergamot, or jasmine and sandalwood.

- Skin Sensitivity: Perform a patch test before using the solid perfume, especially if you have sensitive skin or allergies to certain scents.

- Shelf Life: Properly stored, the solid perfume can last for several months to a year, depending on the oils used.

THIS HOMEMADE SOLID perfume offers a natural and portable way to enjoy your favorite scents. It can be produced in small quantities for personal use or potentially as part of a small-scale production setup. Adjust the recipe according to your preferred fragrance blends and scent intensity.

Ingredients:

Castile Soap - 1/2 cup (liquid form)

Water - 1/2 cup

White Vinegar - 2 tablespoons

Super Washing Soda - 1 tablespoon (optional, for added cleaning power)

Essential Oils - 10-15 drops (optional, for fragrance and antibacterial properties)

Equipment/Tools:

- Mixing bowl or container
- Spoon or whisk for mixing
- Bottle or container for storage

Method:

Prepare Your Workspace:

- Ensure your workspace is clean and dry. Gather the tools and ingredients needed.

Mix the Ingredients:

- In a mixing bowl or container, combine the castile soap and water. Mix thoroughly until well combined.

Add Vinegar and Washing Soda (Optional):

- Add the white vinegar and, if using, the super washing soda to the soap and water mixture. Stir until everything is fully dissolved and mixed.

Add Essential Oils (Optional):

- If desired, add 10-15 drops of essential oils to the mixture for fragrance and antibacterial properties. Stir again to distribute the oils evenly.

Transfer to Storage Container:

- Pour the homemade dishwashing liquid into a bottle or container suitable for storage.

Label and Store:

- Label the container with the date of preparation and contents.Store it in a cool, dry place.

Additional Tips:

- Usage: Use this homemade dishwashing liquid as you would any commercial dish soap. Pour a small amount onto a sponge or directly into the sink to wash dishes.

- Adjustments: You can adjust the essential oil quantities for a preferred scent or add more water if you find the mixture too thick.

This DIY dishwashing liquid is an eco-friendly alternative to store-bought options and can effectively clean dishes. However, note that it might not produce as much foam as commercial detergents due to the absence of certain chemicals used for foaming agents. Adjust the ingredients to suit your preferences and cleaning needs.

Ingredients:

Castile Soap - 2 cups (grated or chopped finely)

Washing Soda - 2 cups

Borax - 2 cups (optional, for added cleaning power)

Essential Oils - 20-30 drops (optional, for fragrance and antibacterial properties)

Equipment/Tools:

- Mixing bowl or container
- Grater or food processor (if using bar soap)
- Spoon or whisk for mixing
- Airtight container for storage

Method:

Prepare Your Workspace:

Be sure your working area is clean and dry. Collect the tools and ingredients.

Grate or Chop Castile Soap:

If using a bar of castile soap, grate it finely with a grater or chop it into pieces. It's also easier to chop everything in a food processor.

Mix the Ingredients:

Combine the grated or chopped castile soap, washing soda, and borax (if using) in a mixing bowl or container. Stir the ingredients together until well-blended.

Add Essential Oils (Optional):

For fragrance and antibacterial properties, add 20-30 drops of essential oils if desired. Stir again to mix the oils evenly.

Store in an Airtight Container:
Put the homemade laundry detergent in an airtight storage container.
Label and Store:
Mark the container with the preparation date and contents.Store it in a cool, dry place.

Additional Tips:

● Usage: When using this homemade laundry detergent for a load of laundry, use about 1-2 tablespoons, depending on the size and dirtiness of the load.

● Adjustments: The essential oil amounts can be adjusted to suit the required scent, or they can be omitted altogether.

THIS DO-IT-YOURSELF laundry detergent provides an environmentally friendly alternative to store-bought laundry detergents and cleans clothes well. But remember, everyone is different in what he or she can tolerate, so do not forget individual sensitivities to ingredients or the need for a patch test. Add or subtract materials according to your taste and washing machine.

Ingredients:

White Vinegar - 2 cups
Water - 2 cups
Hair Conditioner - 1 cup (choose a scent you like)
Essential Oils - 10-15 drops (optional, for additional fragrance)

Equipment/Tools:

- Mixing bowl or container
- Whisk or spoon for mixing
- Airtight container for storage

Method:

Prepare Your Workspace:
Make sure your work space is clean and dry. Assemble the tools and ingredients you need.

Mix the Ingredients:

White vinegar and water are combined in a mixing bowl or container. Mix them together thoroughly.

Add Hair Conditioner:

Pour in the hair conditioner. This will soften the fabric. Stir well with the vinegar and water mixture to make sure it is evenly dispersed.

Optional: Add Essential Oils:

If preferred, add 10-15 drops of essential oils for greater fragrance. Stir again to help distribute the oils.

Transfer to Storage Container:

Pour the homemade fabric softener into a sealable storage container.

Label and Store:

Write the date of preparation and contents on the container. Place it in a cool, dry place.

Additional Tips:

- Usage: This homemade fabric softener can be used as about 1/4 cup, per load, during the rinse cycle.

- Adjustments: You can increase or decrease the amount of essential oil depending on your taste, or leave them out altogether.

A NATURAL REPLACEMENT for commercial fabric softeners, this DIY fabric softener can smooth clothes without resorting to harsh chemicals. Patch test on a small amount of fabric to ensure the laundry is compatible, to prevent staining, or to avoid the reaction. Adjust the ingredients to suit your personal taste.

Ingredients:

White Vinegar - 1 cup

Water - 1 cup

Lemon Peels - from 1-2 lemons (optional, for added fragrance and cleaning power)

Essential Oils - 10-15 drops (optional, for additional antibacterial properties and fragrance)

Equipment/Tools:

- Glass jar or container with airtight lid for infusion
- Spray bottle for the cleaner
- Funnel (optional)

Method:

Prepare Your Workspace:

Ensure your workspace is clean and dry. Gather the tools and ingredients needed.

Prepare Lemon-Infused Vinegar (Optional):

FILL A GLASS JAR OR container with the white vinegar. Add the lemon peels to the vinegar, covering them completely. Close the jar tightly and let it sit for about a week. This infuses the vinegar with lemon, providing a natural citrus fragrance and boosting its cleaning properties.

Mix the Ingredients:

AFTER INFUSING THE vinegar (if using lemon), combine 1 cup of the infused vinegar or regular white vinegar with 1 cup of water in a mixing bowl or container.

Add Essential Oils (Optional):

IF DESIRED, ADD 10-15 drops of essential oils to the vinegar and water mixture for added antibacterial properties and fragrance. Stir the mixture to combine.

Transfer to Spray Bottle:

If necessary, use a funnel to pour the homemade all-purpose cleaner into a spray bottle for easy use.

Label and Store:

Write on the spray bottle what the liquid is and the date of its preparation. Store it in a cool, dry place and away from direct sunlight.

Additional Tips:

- Usage: This homemade all-purpose cleaner can be used on a variety of surfaces, including countertops, sinks and tiles. Shake well before each use.

- Adjustments: Even the amount of essential oils can be adjusted for smell; or you can skip them altogether.

THIS DIY ALL-PURPOSE cleaner provides a homemade, natural and effective replacement for commercial cleaners, and can be used for many household cleaning chores. Before using the product on delicate surfaces, always do a spot test in some inconspicuous area to determine its compatibility. Adjust ingredients to suit your taste.

Ingredients:

- White Vinegar - 1 cup
- Rubbing Alcohol (Isopropyl Alcohol) - 1 cup
- Water - 1 cup
- Cornstarch - 1 tablespoon (optional, for added cleaning power)
- Essential Oils - 5-10 drops (optional, for fragrance)

Equipment/Tools:

- Spray bottle for the cleaner
- Funnel (optional)

Method:

Prepare Your Workspace:

Keep your workspace clean and dry. Collect the implements and materials.

Mix the Ingredients:

Put the white vinegar, rubbing alcohol and water in a bowl or container. Mix the ingredients well to ensure they are thoroughly mixed.

Optional: Add Cornstarch:

Optionally, 1 tablespoon of cornstarch can be added to the mixture. Sometimes cornstarch can help to remove the stubborn stains and grime on glass surfaces. Stir until the cornstarch dissolves.

Optional: Add Essential Oils:

For a fragrant aroma, add 5-10 drops of essential oils, if desired. Stir again to mix the oils together evenly.

Transfer to Spray Bottle:

USE A FUNNEL IF NECESSARY to carefully pour the homemade glass cleaner into a spray bottle for easy application.

Label and Store:

LABEL THE SPRAY BOTTLE with the contents and date of preparation. Store it in a cool, dry place away from direct sunlight.

Additional Tips:

- Usage: Use this homemade glass cleaner on windows, mirrors, and glass surfaces. Spray the cleaner onto the surface and wipe it clean with a lint-free cloth or paper towels for streak-free results.

- Adjustments: You can adjust the quantity of essential oils for a preferred scent or skip them altogether.

THIS DIY GLASS CLEANER offers a natural and effective alternative to commercial glass cleaners, suitable for various glass surfaces around the home. Always perform a spot test in an inconspicuous area before using it on delicate surfaces to ensure compatibility. Adjust the ingredients according to your preferences.

Ingredients:

- Baking Soda - 1 cup

- White Vinegar - 1 cup

- Essential Oils - 10-15 drops (optional, for fragrance and added cleaning properties)

- Liquid Dish Soap - 1 tablespoon (optional, for extra cleaning power)

Equipment/Tools:

- Mixing bowl or container
- Toilet brush or scrubber

Method:

Prepare Your Workspace:

Ensure your workspace is clean and dry. Gather the tools and ingredients needed.

Mix the Ingredients:

IN A MIXING BOWL OR container, combine the baking soda and white vinegar. The mixture will fizz initially; this reaction helps to clean and deodorize.

Optional: Add Essential Oils and Dish Soap:

IF DESIRED, ADD 10-15 drops of essential oils for fragrance and added cleaning power. You can add an extra tablespoon of liquid dish soap if you wish to increase its cleaning power. Mix thoroughly to fully incorporate all the ingredients.

Apply to the Toilet Bowl:

Pour the home brewed toilet bowl cleaner straight into the toilet bowl, covering the sides as much as possible.

Scrub and Let Sit:

Scrub the cleaner around the bowl with a toilet brush or scrubber, making sure to get under the rim. For better effectiveness, let the cleaner sit in the bowl for about 15-20 minutes.

Scrub Again and Flush:

Let the cleaner sit for a while and then scrub the bowl with the brush or scrubber again. Rinse the cleaner off by flushing the toilet.

Additional Tips:

- Usage: So this is a homemade toilet bowl cleaner which can be used as required for cleaning. It aids with stains and takes the smell out of the toilet bowl.

- Adjustments: You can adjust the amount of essential oils for your preferred scent, or leave them out altogether.

THIS HOMEMADE TOILET bowl cleaner is a natural and effective substitute for commercial cleaners, and it really cleans and deodorizes toilet bowls. According to your taste, alter them accordingly and it will serve as a daily cleaner, keeping the toilet bowl clean and fresh.

Ingredients:

- Baking Soda - 1 cup

- Cornstarch - 1 cup

- Bay Leaves - 2-3 leaves (optional, for fragrance)

- Essential Oils - 10-15 drops (optional, for fragrance and added cleaning properties)

Equipment/Tools:

- Mixing bowl or container
- Sifter or fine mesh strainer
- Vacuum cleaner

Method:

Prepare Your Workspace:

Ensure your workspace is clean and dry. Gather the tools and ingredients needed.

Mix the Dry Ingredients:

IN A MIXING BOWL OR container, combine the baking soda and cornstarch. Stir or whisk the mixture to ensure it's well blended.

Optional: Add Fragrance with Bay Leaves and Essential Oils:

IF DESIRED, CRUSH 2-3 bay leaves and mix them into the baking soda and cornstarch mixture. This can add a natural fragrance. Additionally, add

10-15 drops of essential oils for added fragrance and cleaning properties. Mix thoroughly to distribute the fragrance evenly.

Apply the Mixture to the Carpet:

SPRINKLE THE HOMEMADE carpet cleaner mixture generously over the carpet, focusing on areas that require cleaning or deodorizing.

Let it Sit:

ALLOW THE MIXTURE TO sit on the carpet for at least 15-20 minutes. This time allows the baking soda and cornstarch to absorb odors and helps loosen dirt.

Vacuum Thoroughly:

USE A VACUUM CLEANER to thoroughly vacuum up the carpet cleaner mixture from the carpet. Ensure you vacuum all treated areas until no residue remains.

Additional Tips:

- Usage: Use this homemade carpet cleaner to freshen and deodorize carpets. It can help absorb odors and lift light stains.

- Adjustments: You can adjust the quantity of essential oils for a preferred scent or skip them altogether.

THIS DIY CARPET CLEANER provides a natural and gentle way to freshen up carpets. It's suitable for routine cleaning and deodorizing. Always perform a patch test in an inconspicuous area to ensure compatibility with your carpet fibers. Adjust the ingredients according to your preferences.

Leather Cleaner and Conditioner

Ingredients:

- White Vinegar - 1/4 cup

- Olive Oil - 1/2 cup

- Essential Oils - 10 drops (optional, for fragrance and additional conditioning)

Equipment/Tools:

- Mixing bowl or container
- Soft cloths or microfiber towels

Method:

Prepare Your Workspace:

Ensure your workspace is clean and dry. Gather the tools and ingredients needed.

Mix the Ingredients:

IN A MIXING BOWL OR container, combine the white vinegar and olive oil. Stir or whisk the mixture thoroughly to blend the ingredients well.

Optional: Add Essential Oils:

IF DESIRED, ADD 10 drops of essential oils to the mixture for a pleasant fragrance and additional conditioning properties. Essential oils like lavender or tea tree can work well.

Transfer to an Applicator:

YOU CAN POUR THE HOMEMADE leather cleaner and conditioner into a spray bottle for easy application or simply use a soft cloth or microfiber towel to apply the mixture directly onto the leather.

How to Use:

- Test the mixture on a small, inconspicuous area of the leather to ensure compatibility.

- Apply a small amount of the cleaner/conditioner to the leather surface.

- Gently rub and massage the mixture onto the leather using circular motions.

- Allow the conditioner to penetrate for a few minutes.

- Buff off any excess conditioner with a clean, dry cloth to restore shine.

Additional Tips:

- Usage: Use this homemade cleaner and conditioner to clean and condition leather furniture, bags, jackets, or other leather items.

- Adjustments: You can adjust the quantity of essential oils for a preferred scent or skip them altogether.

THIS DIY LEATHER CLEANER and conditioner offer a natural and gentle way to clean and condition leather items. Always test in a hidden area first to ensure compatibility and to avoid any adverse reactions. Adjust the ingredients according to your preferences and the needs of your leather items.

Leather Cleaner and Conditioner

Ingredients:

- White Vinegar - 1/4 cup

- Olive Oil - 1/2 cup

- Essential Oils - 10 drops (optional, for fragrance and additional conditioning)

Equipment/Tools:

- Mixing bowl or container
- Soft cloths or microfiber towels

Method:

Prepare Your Workspace:

Ensure your workspace is clean and dry. Gather the tools and ingredients needed.

Mix the Ingredients:

IN A MIXING BOWL OR container, combine the white vinegar and olive oil. Stir or whisk the mixture thoroughly to blend the ingredients well.

Optional: Add Essential Oils:

IF DESIRED, ADD 10 drops of essential oils to the mixture for a pleasant fragrance and additional conditioning properties. Essential oils like lavender or tea tree can work well.

Transfer to an Applicator:

YOU CAN POUR THE HOMEMADE leather cleaner and conditioner into a spray bottle for easy application or simply use a soft cloth or microfiber towel to apply the mixture directly onto the leather.

How to Use:

- Test the mixture on a small, inconspicuous area of the leather to ensure compatibility.

- Apply a small amount of the cleaner/conditioner to the leather surface.

- Gently rub and massage the mixture onto the leather using circular motions.

- Allow the conditioner to penetrate for a few minutes.

- Buff off any excess conditioner with a clean, dry cloth to restore shine.

Additional Tips:

- Usage: Use this homemade cleaner and conditioner to clean and condition leather furniture, bags, jackets, or other leather items.

- Adjustments: You can adjust the quantity of essential oils for a preferred scent or skip them altogether.

THIS DIY LEATHER CLEANER and conditioner offer a natural and gentle way to clean and condition leather items. Always test in a hidden area first to ensure compatibility and to avoid any adverse reactions. Adjust the ingredients according to your preferences and the needs of your leather items.

Ingredients:

- Baking Soda - 1/4 cup
- White Vinegar - 1/4 cup
- Lemon Juice - 1 tablespoon
- Cornstarch - 1 tablespoon (optional, for added polishing power)
- Water - Enough to create a paste

Equipment/Tools:

- Mixing bowl or container
- Soft cloth or sponge
- Small container for storage

Method:

Prepare Your Workspace:

Ensure your workspace is clean and dry. Gather the tools and ingredients needed.

Mix the Ingredients:

IN A MIXING BOWL OR container, combine the baking soda, white vinegar, lemon juice, and cornstarch (if using). Gradually add water and mix well until you achieve a paste-like consistency.

Apply the Polish:

USE A SOFT CLOTH OR sponge to apply the homemade metal polish onto the metal surface you want to clean and polish.

Polishing:

GENTLY RUB THE PASTE onto the metal surface using circular motions. Apply a little pressure on areas with tarnish or stains.

Rinse and Dry:

ONCE YOU'VE FINISHED polishing, rinse the metal surface with water to remove the paste residue.

Dry the surface thoroughly with a clean, dry cloth.

Storage:

STORE ANY LEFTOVER homemade metal polish in a sealed container for future use.

Additional Tips:

- Usage: This homemade metal polish works well on various metals like stainless steel, brass, copper, and chrome. It helps to remove tarnish, stains, and restore shine.

- Adjustments: You can adjust the consistency of the paste by adding more water or baking soda to achieve the desired thickness.

ALWAYS TEST THE HOMEMADE metal polish on a small, inconspicuous area first to ensure it doesn't damage or scratch the metal surface. Adjust the ingredients according to your preferences and the specific needs of the metal you're polishing.

Ingredients:

- White Vinegar - Sufficient amount to cover the rusty area
- Baking Soda - Optional, for extra abrasive power
- Steel Wool or Scrubbing Pad - For scrubbing (if needed)
- Water - For rinsing

Equipment/Tools:

- Container or basin large enough to submerge the rusty item
- Gloves (for protection)
- Soft cloth or sponge
- Protective eyewear (optional)

Method:

Prepare Your Workspace:

Ensure your workspace is well-ventilated and lay down protective coverings as vinegar can have a strong smell.

Submerge the Rusty Item:

PLACE THE RUSTY ITEM in a container or basin and pour enough white vinegar to completely cover the rusted areas. Allow it to soak for several hours or overnight. For larger items or severe rust, you may need to extend the soaking time.

Scrubbing (if necessary):

AFTER SOAKING, USE a steel wool pad or a scrubbing sponge to gently scrub away the loosened rust. If needed, sprinkle baking soda onto the rusty areas to add an abrasive element to the scrubbing process.

Rinse and Dry:

RINSE THE ITEM THOROUGHLY with water to remove the vinegar and any remaining rust particles.

Dry the item completely using a soft cloth to prevent further rusting.

Additional Tips:

- Usage: This homemade rust remover is suitable for smaller items or surfaces affected by light to moderate rust. For larger or heavily rusted items, you might need multiple treatments or professional assistance.

- Safety Precautions: Wear gloves and protective eyewear while working with rust removers to protect your skin and eyes.

ALWAYS TEST THE HOMEMADE rust remover on a small area first, especially on delicate or valuable items, to ensure it doesn't cause damage. Adjust the soaking time and intensity of scrubbing based on the severity of the rust. For extensive rust or valuable items, it's advisable to seek professional help to avoid any damage.

Ingredients and Materials:

- Beeswax - Around 1-2 ounces per wrap

- Jojoba Oil or Coconut Oil - Optional, around 1 teaspoon per ounce of beeswax (for added flexibility)

- 100% Cotton Fabric - Choose lightweight, breathable fabric in desired sizes

- Parchment Paper or Silicone Baking Mat

- Grater or Beeswax Pellets

- Baking Sheet

- Clothesline or Drying Rack

Method:

Cut Fabric to Size:

Cut the cotton fabric into desired sizes and shapes for your wraps. Common sizes are around 10x10 inches or 12x12 inches, but you can adjust based on your needs.

Prepare Work Area:

COVER YOUR WORK SURFACE with parchment paper or a silicone baking mat to protect it from melted wax.

Melt the Beeswax:

PREHEAT YOUR OVEN TO around 175°F (80°C). Grate the beeswax or use beeswax pellets and spread an even layer over a baking sheet lined with parchment paper.

Bake the Beeswax:

PLACE THE BAKING SHEET with the beeswax into the preheated oven. Allow it to melt completely (about 5-10 minutes).

Add Oil (Optional):

IF DESIRED, YOU CAN add a teaspoon of jojoba oil or coconut oil per ounce of melted beeswax for added flexibility. Mix well.

Apply Wax to Fabric:

LAY A PIECE OF FABRIC flat on the prepared surface. Using a brush or the back of a spoon, evenly spread the melted beeswax mixture over the fabric, covering it entirely.

Remove Excess Wax:

LIFT THE FABRIC AND let excess wax drip off. You can use the brush to even out the wax or redistribute it if needed.

Set and Dry:

HANG THE WAX-COATED fabric on a clothesline or drying rack to air dry and set. It should dry within a few minutes.

Repeat for Multiple Wraps:

REPEAT THE PROCESS for additional fabric pieces until all are coated with wax.

Usage Tips:

- Storage: Store your beeswax wraps in a cool, dry place away from heat sources. They can be folded or rolled for storage.

- Maintenance: To clean, simply wash them with mild soap and cool water. Avoid hot water or heat sources that can melt the wax.

BEESWAX WRAPS ARE A reusable and eco-friendly alternative to plastic wrap for food storage. Experiment with different fabrics and sizes to suit your needs. Adjust the amount of wax to achieve the desired level of stiffness or flexibility in the wraps.